Stories
from the
Amazon

by
Saviour Pirotta

Illustrated by
Rebecca Gryspeerdt

WAYLAND

OTHER MULTICULTURAL STORIES:

 Stories from CHINA

Stories from INDIA

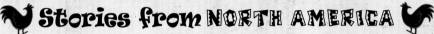 Stories from NORTH AMERICA

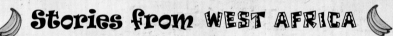 Stories from THE CARIBBEAN

Stories from WEST AFRICA

Series Editor: Paul Mason (paulm@wayland.co.uk)
Art Director: Jane Hawkins
Designer: Tessa Barwick
Production controller: Carol Titchener
Printer/binder: G. Canale & C. S.p.A.

First published in 1999 by
Wayland Publishers Ltd
61 Western Rd
BN3 1JD, England.
www.wayland.co.uk

British Library Cataloguing in Publication Data
Pirotta, Saviour, 1958–
Stories From The Amazon
1.Tales - Amazon - Juvenile literature
I.Title II.Gryspeerdt, Rebecca
398.2'0981
ISBN 0 7502 2423 1

Contents

Introduction

Like many other people, I became interested in the Amazon rain forest when its destruction was first highlighted by the media a few years ago. Before that I had only been vaguely aware of it. I knew jaguars lived there, and vampire bats. But I never really thought much about it or its value to our planet.

Then I saw a programme on the telly about mining for gold in the Amazon rivers. I was horrified by the images of thoughtless destruction. Rivers were being polluted. Plants, fish and animals were being pushed to the brink of extinction. And that wasn't all. Farmers were destroying the forest to make way for farmland. The tribal people who lived there were losing their homes. The world was losing one of its richest assets.

When you are on the verge of losing something, you immediately become aware of how precious it is. Suddenly I found myself reading avidly about the rain forest in general and the Amazon in particular. I found out some mind-boggling facts: at four million square kilometres the Amazon is the biggest rain forest in the world. The Amazon river is 6,500 kilometres long and is home to 2,500 species of fish. Countless animals, insects and plants, many of which we don't know much about, live in the land around it.

This book and its stories are a celebration of the Amazon rain forest, its peoples, cultures and treasures. I hope it will make many of you aware how wonderful it is and how important it is to save before it is lost.

Saviour.

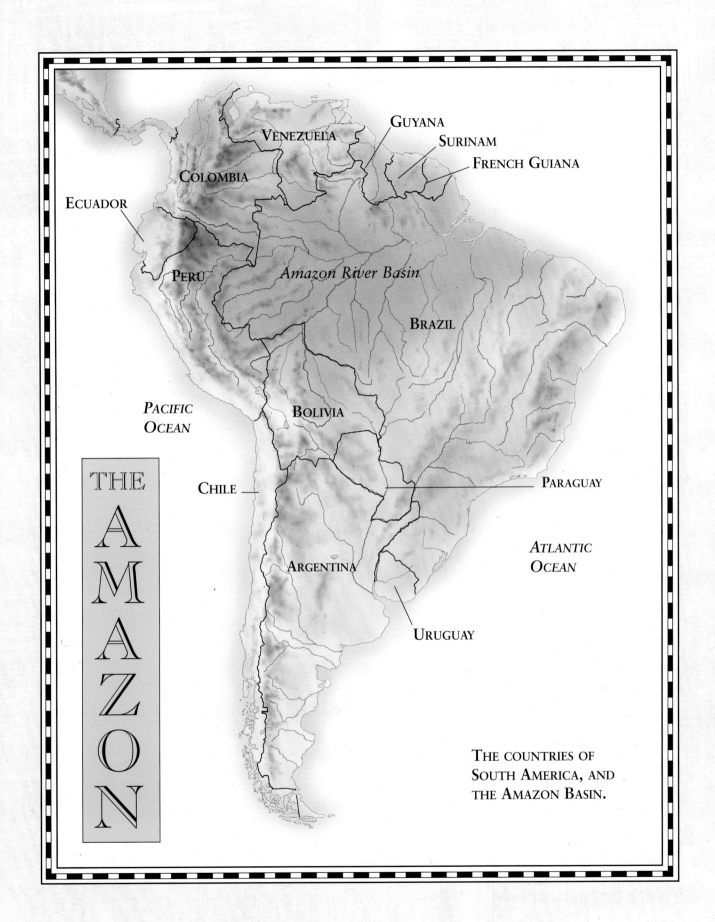

VENEZUELA

GUYANA

SURINAM

FRENCH GUIANA

COLOMBIA

ECUADOR

PERU

Amazon River Basin

BRAZIL

PACIFIC OCEAN

BOLIVIA

CHILE

PARAGUAY

ATLANTIC OCEAN

ARGENTINA

URUGUAY

THE AMAZON

THE COUNTRIES OF
SOUTH AMERICA, AND
THE AMAZON BASIN.

HOW THE WORLD BEGAN

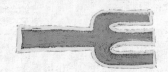

Almost all peoples try to explain the creation of the world around them through myths and legends. We also use stories to show how gods brought order out of chaos, how the first people came to the world and how they learnt the first tasks of civilization.

The peoples of the Amazon have many creation myths. The Yanomami tell of Omam, a bird-like god who created the world, the forest and all the plants and living creatures in it. Meanwhile, the Trio people of Brazil have a story about Waraku. She was the spirit of a fish, who taught a fisherman called Paraparawa how to grow yams and potatoes, how to make tools, utensils and bread, and how to cook.

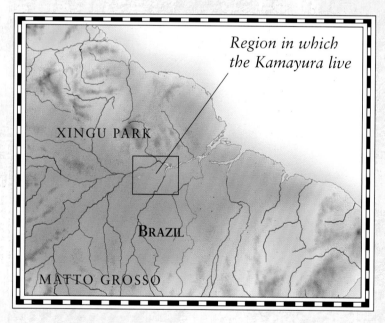

Region in which the Kamayura live

XINGU PARK

BRAZIL

MATTO GROSSO

The creation story that starts on the next page is told by the Kamayura people, who live in the forests of Brazil.

This region is in the north-east of Brazil, near the mouth of the Amazon.

The Legend of the Sun God

In the beginning there was no light in the forest. All the sun's golden rays were caught up in the Kingdom Of The Birds, high above the trees. The people woke up in the dark and went to bed in the dark. They could never see anything around them.

'This is most unfair,' said Kuat, the sun god. 'I want everyone to enjoy the light.'

'It's that Urubutsin, the king of the vultures,' sighed his brother Iae, who was the moon god. 'He's knitted the tops of the trees together so that no light shines on the ground.'

'Well,' said Kuat, 'I'm going to set things right. You just watch me.'

He looked down at the world. The people were stumbling around in the darkness, banging their heads against trees and tripping over roots. 'I must lure Urubutsin down there,' he thought. 'He shall see for himself what it is like to live in darkness.'

Kuat spied a dead body lying on the river bank. Its eyes shone bright white in the dark. Something was crawling all over its decaying skin – a mass of hungry maggots.

Kuat called for the king of the flies. 'Get your subjects to settle on that body,' he ordered, 'tell them to make as much noise as they can.'

The flies settled on the body. They flapped their wings to make as much noise as possible. Urubutsin, who was sitting in the trees, noticed them right away.

'What are those flies feasting on?' he wondered.

He flew down to have a look. The flies scattered, leaving the corpse for the vulture.

Urubutsin landed on the dead man's chest. He picked out the eyes with his beak and gobbled them up. Then he started on the flesh.

'Do you like it?' asked the king of the flies.

'Yes,' said Urubutsin.

'It's a present from Kuat, the sun god,' said the king of the flies. 'Tomorrow he might send you another one.'

'In that case,' said Urubutsin, 'I shall be back around lunch time.' He flew off into the trees. He would have licked his lips, if vultures had lips.

The king of the flies reported back to Kuat. Kuat told the flies to find another body. They were to move it to the banks of the river, where Urubutsin was sure to see it.

That night, Kuat slipped through the trees down to the ground. The forest smelt damp and musty. Everything around him seemed to be festering. There were no flowers or butterflies, only mushrooms and frogs and scorpions looking

for food. Kuat slipped inside the dead body and lay very still. The maggots, sensing his presence, scattered. But Kuat willed them back. The next day at lunch time, the flies returned.

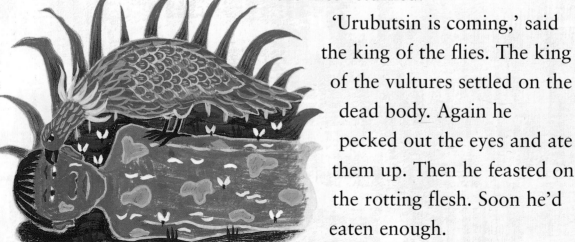

'Urubutsin is coming,' said the king of the flies. The king of the vultures settled on the dead body. Again he pecked out the eyes and ate them up. Then he feasted on the rotting flesh. Soon he'd eaten enough.

'I must tell my subjects about this,' said Urubutsin out loud. He spread his wings to fly. But just then Kuat reached out and grabbed him by the foot. Urubutsin screamed.

'Let me go,' he snarled.

'No,' said Kuat, 'I want you to stay here forever, where it is dark and damp.'

'I am a bird,' argued Urubutsin. 'I was made to fly in the light.'

'The people too are meant to be in the light,' said Kuat, 'but you have condemned them to live in the dark.'

The king of the vultures flapped his wings, trying to escape.

'I shall not let go,' warned Kuat, 'until you promise to let the sun shine down into the forest.'

'I shall never do that,' said Urubutsin.

'Very well, then,' laughed Kuat. 'Stay here in the dark forever.' Urubutsin made one last attempt to escape but he knew that Kuat was too powerful for him.

'I give in,' he screeched, 'Let me go and I shall let light into the forest.'

'No,' said Kuat, 'Let the light in first.'

The king of the vultures summoned his minions. 'Let the
light shine into the forest,' he commanded. The birds flew
up into the trees and ripped the branches of the trees apart
with their beaks. The sun's light shone down on the forest.
The people were blinded at first. Then they held their faces
up to receive the sun's warmth.

And ever since then, the sun's light has shone in the
forest every day.

FLOODS & DISASTERS

It seems that every culture on Earth has a story about the world being submerged under water. In the rain forest, the Ipurina people tell of Mayuruberu, the chief of the storks. He caused a flood when he forgot that he had put his kettle on the sun to boil and it overflowed. The Tupi people believe in Monan. He made the world, but destroyed it with fire and tidal waves before rebuilding it again.

Many flood myths follow the same pattern as the story of Noah's flood in the Bible. The first people do something that angers their god. God sends a flood to wipe them out. But a handful of good people survive. They start a new, and better, world.

In the Amazon, parts of the forest flood every year. The floods destroy, but they also bring new life by spreading seeds.

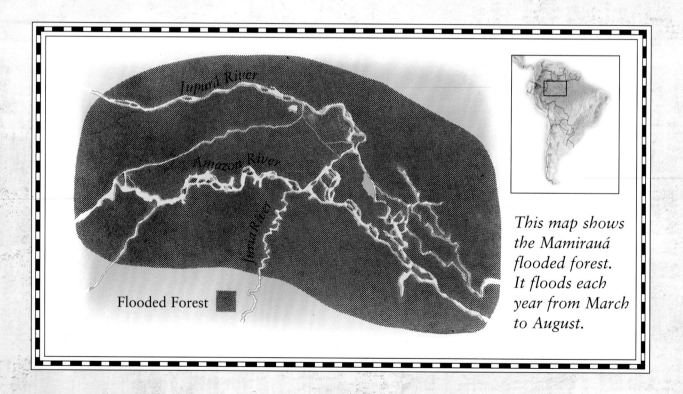

Jupurá River

Amazon River

Jurua River

Flooded Forest

This map shows the Mamirauá flooded forest. It floods each year from March to August.

The Tree of Life

Back at the start of time, the forest was a different place. All the first people had to eat was leaves, or berries.

Agouti walked through the forest. He'd been searching for something tasty to eat but yet again he'd found nothing except leaves and berries.

I don't know how long Agouti walked, but at last he came to a part of the forest he had never seen before. He could smell something in the air, something sweet and tangy. It made his mouth water. Agouti followed his nose. He kept on walking and walking till at last he stood in front of a great tree, with branches that seemed to reach right into the big blue sky.

'Dear me!' cried Agouti. The tree was covered in every kind of fruit you can imagine: apricots, bananas, coconuts, dates, oranges. You name it – it was hanging there.

Agouti climbed into the branches and started eating. 'I shall not tell anyone about this tree,' he said to himself, 'I shall keep all this fruit for myself.'

A week later Agouti's brother, who was called Macounaima, said to his friends and his other brothers: 'Have you noticed how fat Agouti is growing?'

'Yes' said the others, 'He must be having something more than leaves and berries to eat.'

Early the next morning, Macounaima slipped out of his hammock. Agouti was already up, his belly rumbling with hunger.

'Good morning,' said Macounaima.

'Morning,' said Agouti. He didn't look at all pleased to see his brother.

'Going to find more berries?' asked Macounaima.

'Yes,' snapped Agouti.

'I shall come with you,' said Macounaima.

'I'd rather go on my own,' mumbled Agouti.

'You are hiding something from me,' said Macounaima. 'You have found something more than leaves and berries to eat. Come on, own up.'

'Alright,' whispered Agouti. 'But if I tell what and where it is, you must promise to keep it a secret.'

'I promise,' said Macounaima.

Agouti led his brother to the giant tree. Macounaima's jaw dropped when he saw all the fruit. 'This is the Tree of Life itself,' he said, 'We can't keep a thing like this to ourselves.' He gathered some fruit and took it back home. All the people in the village had a taste.

'Where did you find all this?' they asked. 'Tell us, so we can get some more.'

'Come,' said Macounaima, 'I'll show you.'

The entire village followed him to the Tree of Life. 'Go away,' said Agouti, who was sitting under the tree, eating bananas, 'this is my tree.'

The villagers ignored him. They started picking the ripe fruit that had fallen to the ground. The children climbed into the lower branches.

'Be careful,' said Agouti, 'we must leave some fruit for tomorrow.'

'Nonsense,' laughed the people, 'the tree will bear more fruit tomorrow.'

More and more children swarmed up the tree. They tore the fruit off the branches and threw it to the ground. Someone poked a wasp's nest. The wasps buzzed angrily. A boy got stung.

'That's it', said his dad. 'Let's chop the tree down before anyone else gets hurt.'

'No!' said Macounaima and Agouti together. But their voices were drowned out by the villagers' laughter. In no time at all, the mighty tree fell over.

Suddenly there was a loud roar. A deluge of icy water burst through the tree stump. Soon the whole forest was drowned. Macounaima and his people had to find shelter on a high mountain, leaving the precious fruit behind them. There they sat for many days, wincing in the heat of the sun.

When at last the water dried, Macounaima led everyone back to the forest. The Tree of Life was nowhere to be seen. But all over the forest were thousands of new trees, each one bearing one kind of fruit. They had grown out of the seeds inside the fruit scattered by the water.

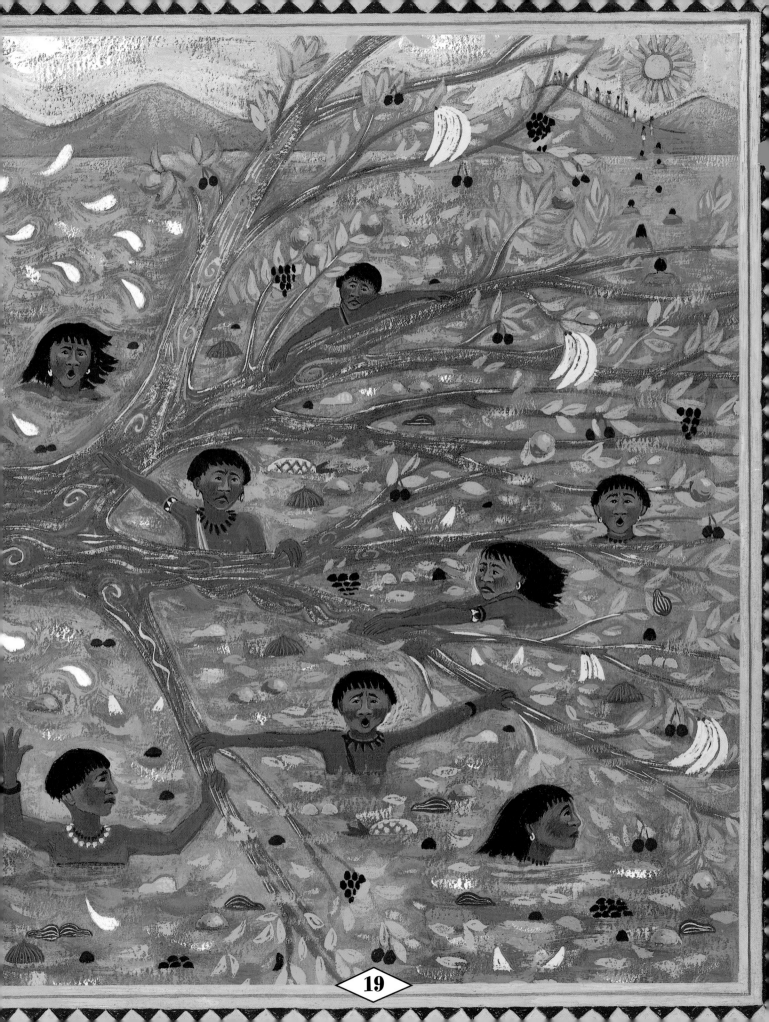

THE AMAZON MIRACLE PLANT

The rain forest is filled with a mind-boggling array of fruits and vegetables, which have sustained the forest peoples for thousands of years. One of these is Guarana.

This Guarana plant's berries are just about ripe.

Guarana was first discovered by the Maues people. They pulped it and made it into a drink. Many farmers have tried to grow Guarana outside the rain forest, but with no success. Even today, when you can buy Guarana gum in a chemist's shop, the best crops still come from the place in which it was first found. And no Guarana grows outside of the Amazon region. The locals say it is a miracle plant. It cures headaches, upset stomachs and sleeplessness, and gives people energy when they're tired.

No wonder there are so many legends about Guarana.

Buried Eyes

The good god Tupa lived in the forest. Every day he looked after the people, making sure that the evil god Jurupari, the lord of the darkness, would not hurt them. The people could not see Tupa, but he blew with the breeze, shone with the sun, twinkled with the stars that peeped out of the heavens. Every day the people came to him with prayers. 'Good Lord Tupa,' they begged, 'let us find enough food to eat, keep the snakes and the jaguars away from our children, heal our wounded hunters.'

One couple, both getting on in years, never asked Tupa for food or pleasant dreams. Instead they repeated the same request over and over again.

'Oh Good God Tupa, give us a child to look after and care for. We'll teach it to love and respect you.'

Tupa looked into the couple's hearts and saw that they would make excellent parents. So he granted their wish.

Some time later the woman had a baby, a chubby little boy with a nose like a button. All the people in the tribe adored him. They brought him presents. When his mother took him down to the river, the girls all helped to bathe him.

The baby grew into a strong, happy boy with big, soft eyes. He was kind and generous too. Everywhere he went, people gathered round to listen to his stories and jokes.

'He is the best hunter in the forest,' said the old men when they sat together talking.

'And the most good looking one too,' sighed the girls. 'He has wonderful eyes.'

'He is the kindest young man we ever met,' said the old women.

'And the bravest fighter,' agreed the boys. 'No one is ever scared when he's around.'

The good god Tupa was very pleased with the boy. But the evil god Jurupari was jealous of him.

'No one thinks of me now,' he moaned, lurking in the deepest, thickest shadows. 'Everyone seems to have forgotten me. I am the fear, the darkness of the night. I am the maker of nightmares and the bringer of the storms.

Yet no one thinks of me anymore as they go to bed. No one shivers at the mention of my name. And it is all this boy's fault. His kindness has banished fear from the forest. I am dying because of him.'

Jurupari turned into a serpent. (The gods can take any shape that they like.) He crawled through the bushes and sneaked into the village. There was the boy, sitting outside the longhouse, surrounded by friends and admirers.

'Tell us a joke,' the children begged the boy, 'sing us a song, a funny one.'

The boy laughed, and the sound of his laughter scattered around the small village like a thousand butterflies. Jurupari winced at the sound, releasing a foul stench from his mouth.

'I must get some fruit for my mother,' said the boy.

'But I'll tell you a story when I get back.'

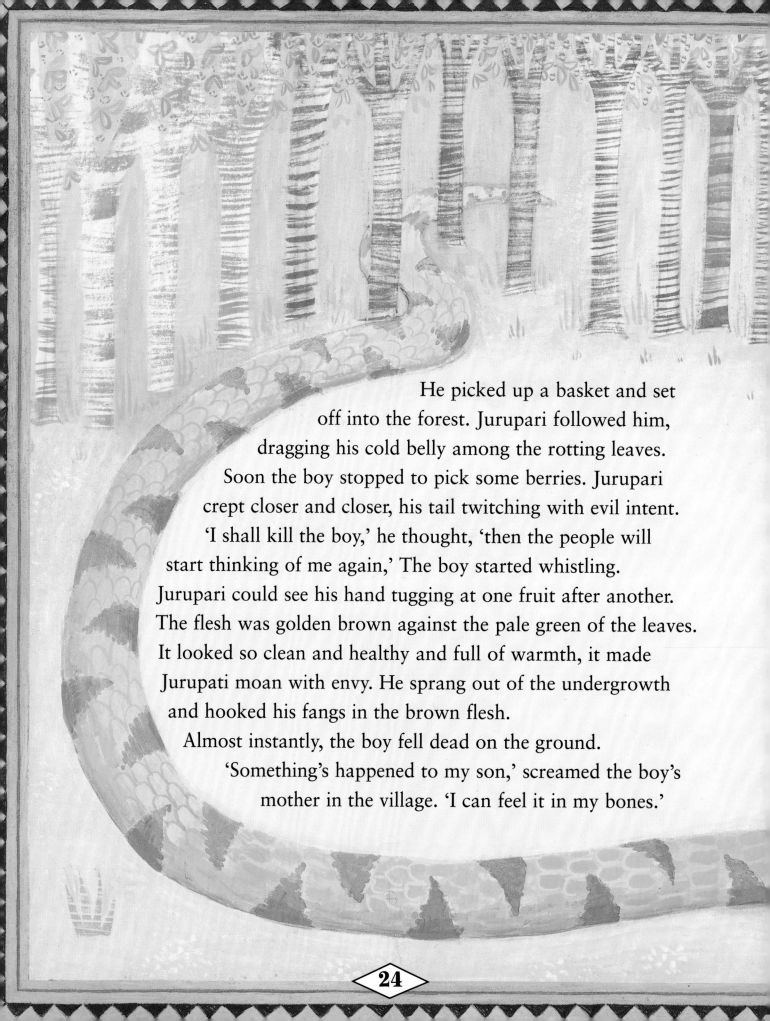

He picked up a basket and set
off into the forest. Jurupari followed him,
dragging his cold belly among the rotting leaves.
Soon the boy stopped to pick some berries. Jurupari
crept closer and closer, his tail twitching with evil intent.
'I shall kill the boy,' he thought, 'then the people will
start thinking of me again,' The boy started whistling.
Jurupari could see his hand tugging at one fruit after another.
The flesh was golden brown against the pale green of the leaves.
It looked so clean and healthy and full of warmth, it made
Jurupati moan with envy. He sprang out of the undergrowth
and hooked his fangs in the brown flesh.
Almost instantly, the boy fell dead on the ground.
'Something's happened to my son,' screamed the boy's
mother in the village. 'I can feel it in my bones.'

People ran to look for the boy. They found him lying on the banks of the river, the colour drained from his cold flesh. His eyes were glassy, the white turned to a dull red. An old woman closed them gently with her hands.

The hunters brought the dead boy into the village and laid him outside the longhouse. Everyone sobbed, cursing the evil Jurupari for his crime. His mother kissed his cold cheeks.

'Why?' she cried, 'Why would the good Tupa give me a son and then let Jurupari take him away from me?' Suddenly a thunderbolt hit the ground beside the longhouse. The woman heard a soft voice whispering in her ear. 'Plant the boy's eyes in the ground,' it said, 'and your son shall never stop looking after you.'

The woman realised that the voice belonged to Tupa. She plucked out the boy's eyes and buried them just where the thunderbolt had struck. The next day she noticed a small bush growing on the spot. Other people noticed it too. They watered it carefully and made sure the snails would not nibble at its leaves.

The bush grew bigger and bigger and soon red berries appeared on its branches. They were the first guarana, the fruit that gives the forest people strength and stamina. The boy's mother picked them and, when they popped open, she discovered large seeds inside. They stared up at her just like the eyes of her son.

THE BOAT PLANT

Many of the amazing trees and plants that grow in the rain forest can't be found anywhere else. One of the strangest is the cannonball tree. Its enormous seeds are as hard as iron, and they drop to the ground with a loud noise that sounds exactly like cannon fire. Then there's the Strangler Fig, a notorious creeper which wraps itself around a tree until it dies. The creeper then takes its victim's place in the sun.

The pads of the Vitoria Regis lily plant are so large that small animals and – some people say – even little children can float on them.

But perhaps the most awe-inspiring rain-forest plant is the record-breaking Vitoria Regis. This is the biggest water lily in the world. Its lily pads are so massive that small animals like rabbits can float across the water on them. This next story is one the rain forest people tell about the Vitoria Regis.

The Sad Song of the Moon

ate every evening, a group of young women went down to the river. They bathed in the warm water, singing beautiful love songs and telling stories. Afterwards they lay on the grass and looked up at the darkening skies.

'How big are the heavens,' one of them would say, 'who knows what wonderful mysteries hide up there?'

'I wish I was a star,' another girl would sigh. 'then I could shoot across the sky and touch the rising moon.'

'We all want to be stars,' the rest of the girls would say, 'then we can live forever.'

One night the girls stayed longer by the river than usual. The evening sky turned jet black and the stars twinkled brighter than normal. The moon was full to bursting point with bright light, casting a silver mantle over the forest.

The girls could not believe their eyes. They had never seen such dazzling splendour before.

The night air was heavy with the scent of tropical flowers. Fireflies danced in the bushes, weaving intricate patterns of green light. The girls felt light-headed, as if they were in a dream. The youngest of the girls, Naia, opened her arms to welcome the light of the full moon. 'How I wish I could touch you,' she whispered. 'Then I too would be filled with your heavenly light.'

The moon, hanging low in the
sky, reached out to caress Naia's face
with its silver rays. She sat up and
looked around.

'What are you looking for?' asked one
of her friends.

'A way to reach the moon,' whispered Naia. 'If I
touch it, it will make me a star.' She stood up and
walked over to a big tree. 'Come on,' she called to
the others, 'follow me.' The girls climbed up to the
very top of the tree. They reached out, their hands
filled with fragrant orchids. But the moon was higher
in the sky than they had expected.

'What a shame,' said one of them, 'now we'll
never become stars.'

The eldest led the way back to the ground. Naia
could not sleep that night. She kept thinking of the
moon, and the soft silver rays that had caressed her
face. 'We must try to reach it before it rises too
high,' she thought.

The next evening the girls did not go down to the river. Instead they climbed up to the top of the highest hill. When the moon rose, they reached out to touch it. But again, it was far too high for them to reach. Disappointed, the girls returned home.

'The moon is out of reach,' said the eldest girl. 'We should stop trying to reach it. Perhaps we are meant to be down here in the forest and not up there in the sky.'

'You are right,' said the other girls, 'let us forget about the moon. Let us think about the boys instead. They are real; they will love us and make us happy.'

But Naia would not give up her dreams. She loved the moon too much. 'I will not marry anyone,' she thought, 'I only want the moon.'

When the rest of the girls were asleep she crept down to the river. It was a still night. There was a only a faint ripple on the surface of the water. Naia sat on the bank and looked up at the sky. The moon seemed to be brighter than usual. Its light touched every flower, every passing moth, filling their petals and wings with light.

'Oh moon, moon,' sighed Naia, 'I cannot come up to you. Why do you not come down to me?' Just then the breeze dropped and the river lay still. Naia saw the moon's reflection on the surface of the water.

'Hello!' she cried, thinking the moon had come down from the skies to see her, 'Wait for me, I'm coming.'

She got to her feet and started walking along the bank of the river. The moon's reflection, of course, moved on before her.

'Wait for me, moon,' called Naia, 'I cannot keep up with you.' At last she stopped walking.

The moon's reflection stopped moving too. It sat out in the middle of the river, where the water was dark and cold and deep. 'I'm coming, moon,' said Naia. She held out her hands and dived into the river. Poor Naia. The cold water made her numb, the weeds grabbed at her feet. She struggled to get to the moon's reflection but the cold water stung her eyes and filled her mouth. Soon the current had dragged her under.

Naia's friends looked for her everywhere. But they could not find her. Instead they found a new plant, floating right in the middle of the river where Naia had drowned. It was a giant lily, pink and fragrant in the morning light. Its beautiful petals were wide open, like Naia's arms trying to catch the moon's light.

'This is the work of the moon,' they said. 'He has changed Naia into a water plant, so that she will always be here, ready to welcome his bright reflection on the water.'

THE PINK DOLPHIN, BUOTO

The waters of the Amazon and Orinoco are home to the Pink Dolphin, known as Buoto by the local people. It is the only dolphin in the world that has a neck. Buotos usually eat small fish and soft crabs. But during the rainy season, when the Amazon floods the forest, they swim around the treetops to nibble at fruit.

The rain forest people have many legends about dolphins. Some people believe that the dolphins were once human beings, who went to live in a golden city at the bottom of the river. Sometimes these magical dolphins remember the lives and friends they once had, and return to land – with dire consequences for the people they meet.

Bufeo Colorado

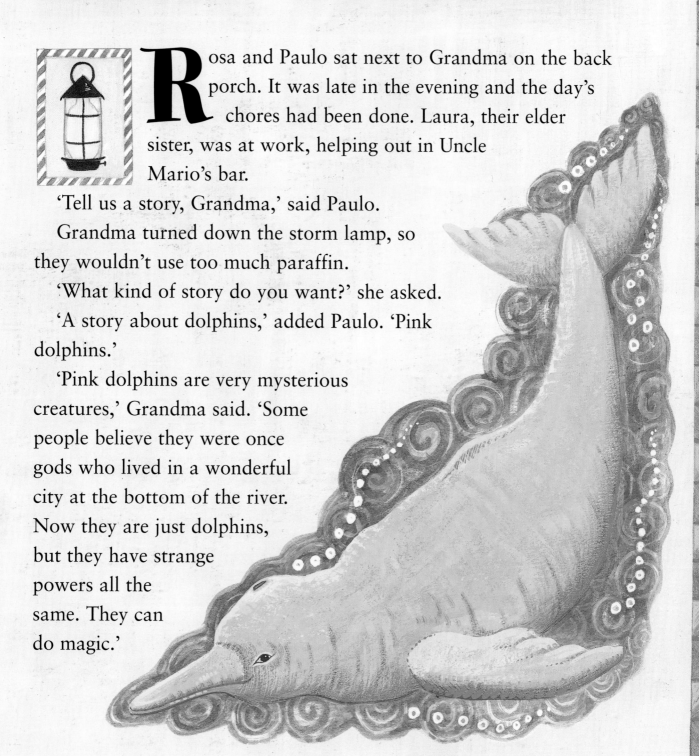

Rosa and Paulo sat next to Grandma on the back porch. It was late in the evening and the day's chores had been done. Laura, their elder sister, was at work, helping out in Uncle Mario's bar.

'Tell us a story, Grandma,' said Paulo.

Grandma turned down the storm lamp, so they wouldn't use too much paraffin.

'What kind of story do you want?' she asked.

'A story about dolphins,' added Paulo. 'Pink dolphins.'

'Pink dolphins are very mysterious creatures,' Grandma said. 'Some people believe they were once gods who lived in a wonderful city at the bottom of the river. Now they are just dolphins, but they have strange powers all the same. They can do magic.'

'What kind of magic?' asked Rosa.

'The leader of the dolphins is called Bufeo Colorado,' whispered Grandma. 'Sometimes, he changes into a man and comes out of the water. He is always dressed smartly in a crisp linen suit. And he always wears a hat on his head. Always.'

'Even when he goes to the toilet?' asked Rosa.

Grandma nodded. 'Bufeo Colorado might be able to change into a very handsome man,' she said, 'but he can't make the blow hole on top of his head disappear. So he hides it under a hat.'

'What does he come to the forest for?' Rosa wanted to know.

'What Bufeo Colorado wants, he wants most of all,' said Grandma, 'and it is to marry a human girl. So he comes to the forest to look for a bride. Just one kiss from the handsome Bufeo and the girl falls under his spell. She follows him into the river and, once she sets eyes on the fabulous city below the waves, she forgets all about her home in the forest. She becomes a pink dolphin herself.'

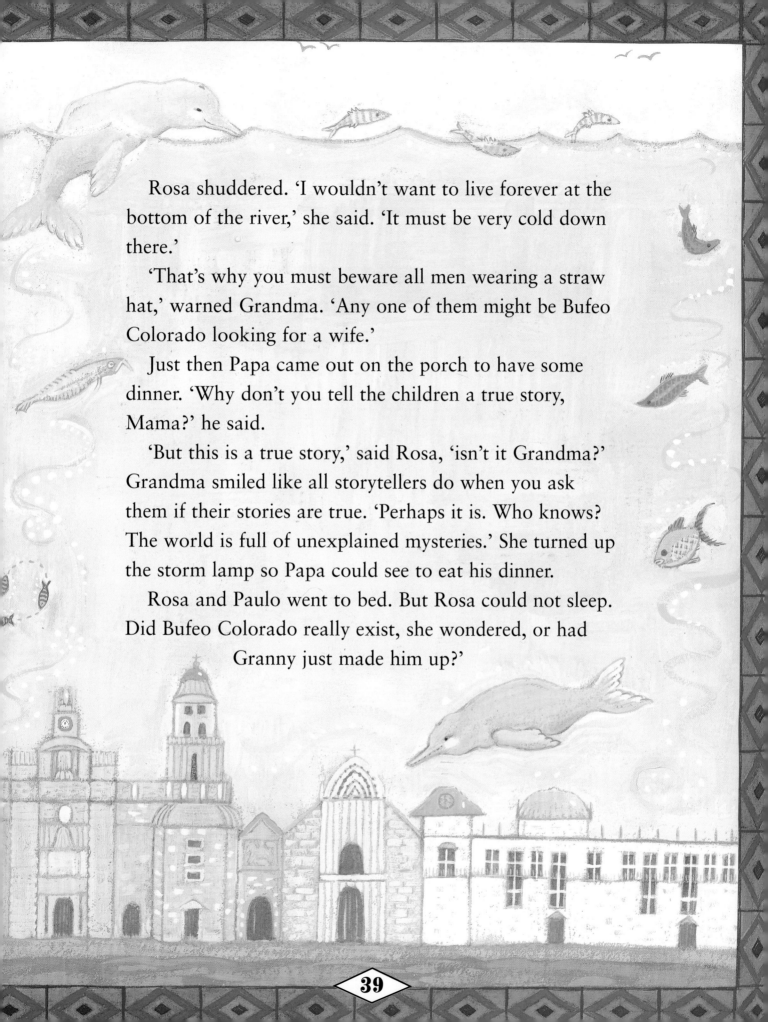

Rosa shuddered. 'I wouldn't want to live forever at the bottom of the river,' she said. 'It must be very cold down there.'

'That's why you must beware all men wearing a straw hat,' warned Grandma. 'Any one of them might be Bufeo Colorado looking for a wife.'

Just then Papa came out on the porch to have some dinner. 'Why don't you tell the children a true story, Mama?' he said.

'But this is a true story,' said Rosa, 'isn't it Grandma?' Grandma smiled like all storytellers do when you ask them if their stories are true. 'Perhaps it is. Who knows? The world is full of unexplained mysteries.' She turned up the storm lamp so Papa could see to eat his dinner.

Rosa and Paulo went to bed. But Rosa could not sleep. Did Bufeo Colorado really exist, she wondered, or had Granny just made him up?'

A week later Rosa and Paulo were fishing on the banks of the river. Suddenly there was a rustle in the bushes behind them. They both turned at once, expecting to see a capybara or a small deer emerging from the undergrowth. Instead they saw a man in a white linen suit. He was terribly handsome. And on his head he wore a straw hat. Paulo and Rosa stiffened.

'Don't be scared of me,' said the man with a smile. 'My name is Carlos. I've come to sell the local ladies some combs. Which way to the town, please?'

'Through there,' said Paulo, pointing to the path they'd used to come from the village.

'No, don't go that way,' interrupted Rosa. 'That's a shortcut only the locals use. You might get lost in the forest. Take the path along the river. It's longer but safer.'

'Thank you,' said the stranger. He started walking along the riverbank, whistling a merry tune.

'That's Bufeo Colorado, isn't it?' whispered Rosa.

'It looks like him,' said Paulo. 'Come on, let's warn the others before he gets to the town.'

They dropped their fishing lines and ran along the shortcut through the bushes. When they got to the village, they burst into Uncle Mario's bar.

'There's a stranger,' stammered Paulo. 'He's...'

'Selling combs to the lovely ladies,' said a familiar voice at one of the tables.

Rosa and Paulo turned on their heels. The stranger was sitting on a bench, drinking tea out of a glass. Somehow he'd made it to the village before them. 'Thank you for showing me the way,' he said. And he took off his hat to fan his face.

Paulo and Rosa stared. There was no blow-hole on top of the man's head. There was only thick, black curly hair, shiny with hair oil.

'We thought you were Bufeo Colorado,' said Paulo, sighing with relief.

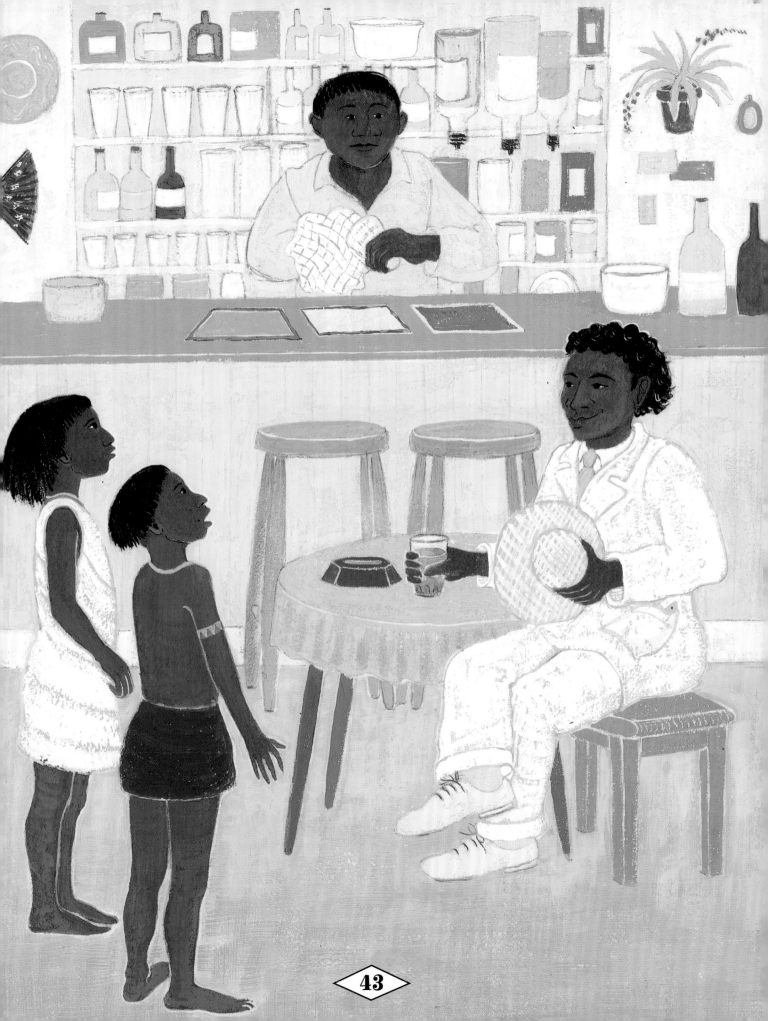

'We thought you might put a spell on our sister Laura,' added Rosa.

The stranger laughed. 'I told you my name is Carlos,' he said. He tossed a couple of coins on the table. 'Give the children an ice-cream, barman. They've been a great help.'

Uncle Mario brought two ice-creams to the table. The man finished his tea and stood up. 'Good afternoon to you all,' he said, heading for the door.

Paulo and Rosa ate their ice-creams slowly, enjoying every single spoonful.

'The man's forgotten his change,' said Uncle Mario when they'd finished, 'Rosa, you go and give it to him. He's staying at the Hotel Splendor.'

Rosa hurried along the deserted street. The Hotel Splendor was right on the other side of town. It was really a converted farmhouse, with an open-air restaurant on the roof. Rosa made her way round to the back of the building. She could hear the stranger singing along with the radio.

'Mister,' she called, looking in through the window.

But the stranger did not hear her. He was standing in front of the mirror, getting ready to shave. As Rosa watched, he took off his hat. Then he took off his HAIR. Rosa realised that the shiny black curls were a wig. The stranger was completely bald. And in the middle of his head he had - a blow hole.

Glossary

Agouti A rat-like creature that lives in the forests and grasslands of South America. It has very strong legs which make it very agile. The boy in our story was called Agouti because he could walk for hours on end without getting tired.

Canopy A sort of platform formed by the branches of rainforest trees growing into each other. It is home to thousands of plants and living creatures but it also stops sunlight from getting through to the forest floor.

Capybara a member of the rat-family that lives on the river banks of the rain forest. It looks like a giant guinea pig and can swim.

Jaguar A ferocious member of the cat family. It is the largest predator in the rain forest, although it rarely attacks people. The people of the Amazon have great respect for the jaguar. Some dress in jaguar pelts for special ceremonies. Others paint jaguar patterns on their faces.

Macounaima In Amazon folk lore, Macounaima is a trickster and a hero. As a child, he was very lazy and got into a lot of scrapes. But people liked his nerve and courage.

Maggots Small, worm-like creatures that turn into flies. They have no legs and live in rotting meat.

Vultures Huge birds that feed on dead meat. They have large wings that help them soar while looking for food. Vultures can tell when a wounded person or animal is going to die and hang about, waiting for their dinner.

Further information

Stories from the Amazon are a bit thin on the ground but *The Kingfisher Book of Mythology* contains some very good short synopses you might be able to use as a basis for retellings. Other stories appear in: *Myths and Legends Around the World*, by Sandy Shepard, Evans Brothers 1994.

Also read:

How Night Came Joanna Troughton (Puffin, 1998).
The Rain Forest Book by Rosalind Kerven (CUP, 1994).

Non-fiction books:

Rain Forest Amerindians, by Anna Lewington (Wayland, 1997)
The Wayland Atlas of Threatened Cultures (Wayland 1997) and *The Wayland Atlas of The Rain Forests* (Wayland 1998)
The World About Us: *Tropical Rain forest* (Watts, 1997)
The Amazon, Michael Pollard (Evans Brothers, 1997)
The Deep In The Rain Forest series (books on animals, plants and trees, people, and rivers) (Wayland 1998)

Websites

Wayland's website address is in the front of this book. Another very useful website belongs to WWF UK: key this into a search engine and you'll be taken straight there. The website links to a variety of others and also contains huge amounts of information.

Rainforest Activities

Communal dancing is a very important part of the rain forest life. Make up a dance drama telling the Legend of the Sun God, which is full of flowing movement. The leading dancers could play Kuat, Urubutsin and Iae. The rest of the class can be the chorus. Their job is to portray the birds, worms and flies. Everyone could wear a mask to show who they are. Alternatively they could paint patterns and symbols on their faces. You can find some good examples of Amazon body painting in the books suggested on page 47.

Make your own **Tree of Life**. Cut out the shape of the tree and pin it up on the wall. Then invite everyone to bring in pictures of fruit cut out of old magazines. How many different kinds of fruit that could be from the rain forest can you paste on the tree?

Flood stories like **The Tree of Life** are very popular all around the world. Imagine there is a flood in your school, then make up a play about it. You could borrow ideas from various flood stories.

Buried Eyes and **The Sad Song of the Moon** are two stories that explain the origin of fruit and plants. Make up your own tales about fruit bought from your local supermarket. The stories could then be made into a book.

Get your class to write reports about sightings of **Bufeo Colorado.** The reports could be collated into a newsletter. Alternatively make a news-report on video. 'Reporters' could speak to the camera and interview 'eye-witnesses'.

Underwater cities have captured the imagination of many writers. Write your own stories about a city at the bottom of the Amazon. Its inhabitants could be some of the characters and animals featured in our stories.